# THE RHYTHM OF LIFE

Edited by

Heather Killingray

First published in Great Britain in 1999 by
ANCHOR BOOKS
Remus House,
Coltsfoot Drive,
Woodston,
Peterborough, PE2 9JX
Telephone (01733) 898101

HB ISBN 1 85930 688 8
SB ISBN 1 85930 683 7

# *FOREWORD*

Anchor Books is a small press, established in 1992, with the aim of promoting readable poetry to as wide an audience as possible.

We hope to establish an outlet for writers of poetry who may have struggled to see their work in print.

The poems presented here have been selected from many entries. Editing proved to be a difficult task and as the Editor, the final selection was mine.

I trust this selection will delight and please the authors and all those who enjoy reading poetry.


Heather Killingray
Editor

# CONTENTS

# No-Man's Land

A strip of land not very wide,
Drawn where opposing generals decide,
Bordered by dense barbed wire,
Behind which entrenched infantry fire,
With minefields strategically located,
This is no-man's land.

Ruined buildings standing deserted,
Occupants the raging battle averted,
Branchless trunks of trees abound,
Leaving no cover on this war-torn ground,
And daylight nothing there a moving,
This is no-man's land.

No wild animal in this land abides,
But at night 'sorties' from both sides,
Then exploding mine as men carelessly lunge,
And into shell holes the living plunge,
Heard once again the call to charge,
This is no-man's land.

Artillery fire and heavy mortar,
Dead horses part of the slaughter,
Last night's bodies hang on the wire,
Ignored by gunners who continue to fire,
Occasional cries from wounded men,
This is no-man's land.

And what of this godless terrain,
Turned to quagmire by the rain,
Rotting corpses strewn around
Friend and foe together found,
And when the final shot is fired,
This is still no-man's land.

*Brian Hodges*

## DON'T GO

Please don't go don't go away
We want you here with us to stay
We want you here to play with us
To roll around and tickle us
We want to sit upon your knee
While you read a book to Jade and me
The book you read we don't care
As long as you're with us sitting there
We want to go on walks with you
Or just sit around and talk to you
And when you tuck us in at night
We feel safe in your arms when you hug us tight
Please don't go don't go away

I don't want to go away anymore
I want to be with the ones I adore
I want to hug and squeeze you tight
And make sure you're safe throughout the night
It makes me sad when I have to go
The feelings I have no one knows
My stomach churns and my heart gets heavy
When I have to leave my babies
I love you more than words can say
More and more with every day
And every day that I'm away
I sit at night and hope and pray
That I'll return all safe and sound
Happy knowing that you're around.

*T Callaghan*

## BEAUTIFUL STAR

Often as I sit I wonder why,
You're so often alone in the sky.
You're always the first at night.
Shining in the heaven so bright.
You're often there, the start of the day,
Although you're beautiful you are far away.
You seem to start from the north,
That's when I see you shining forth.
Maybe you're the star that travelled that night,
And gave the shepherds your guiding light.
To tell them Mary's baby son was born,
In a stable alone and forlorn.
And help the three wise men with gifts to bare,
And people who had love to share.
But beautiful star you still are bright,
And still guide so many with your lovely light.

*Margaret Upson*

## MONDAY

January nights draw in at 4pm.
I stop reading, put the book aside.
In the kitchen, radio voices
too excited for my weariness.
I haven't slept too well for several nights
despite hot chocolate and continental
biscuits when the foxes cry.

Thoughts of tomorrow brighten me.
I take another sip of Belgian beer
and chew another unlit cigarette.
I watch my wife intently working,
her quick hands; scratchy, busy sounds.

She looks over her glasses and smiles,
and my heart shrugs and I'm OK.

*David O'Callaghan*

## THE RAGE AFTER AN ARGUMENT

I thought perhaps you were different for me.
Sharing together our special dreams to be happy.
I willingly gave you the secret key to my heart.
Gone false promises, distant hope, an emptiness to depart.
The rage after an argument, was it a decision right or wrong?
We are both stubborn, can't seem to agree to get on long,
My feelings are mixed, the differences we have,
not a certainty anymore.
The pain between us, an evil experience hurts us both deeply sore.
Difficult times shared together, we can't continue this way.
Us we argued virtually it seemed every alternate weekday.
Now we communicate, with suggestions, the right direction to turn,
For us better days, more understanding, much happiness to churn.
I still remember the day, you showed for me that you really cared.
A special person with fond memories we both shared.
Together now our life has changed, times are happier not like they
used to be.
We realise in the heat of a debate it's not all you or me.
Gone the tempers, the rage, once again we enjoy our old fun.
I can now explain, why I wanted to turn and run,
Or suddenly burst into sobbing distressed tears.
With you on my side, together we can alleviate our frightened fears.
Together, we can search to find the person we both lost.
A gift of special caring. Love is our trusting high ransomed cost.
Still it's easier for you to say 'I love you.'
Once hidden behind a dark mask, I can now say honest 'I do to.'
Past gone these days of darkness, shining a future light,
I need you my knight of shiny armour to make my days again bright.
Yes it's you. The person I feel in love with, the person I used to know.

*Yvonne Fraser*

# IF ONLY I WERE A TOOL BOX

If only I were a tool box, I would build you a home,
it would be so clean, so smart
if only I were a tool box
I would make a start.
If only I were a tool box, I would build our daughter a wendy house,
so she could play,
Whether it be December or May.
If only I were a tool box, I would build our son a tree house,
where he could be with his friends,
and if he were in trouble for something he had done,
he could hide out of sight of his dad and his mom.
His little tree house, his domain and if he were
to cut his finger on it, I'd put on a plaster
of love to ease the pain.
If only I were a tool box, I would rebuild your heart,
but we hide from each other, now we're apart.

If only I were a tool box I could make a start.
I wonder where it is?
O yes it's right here, where it's always been,
right here in my heart.

Me, Myself and I.

*Ian Stuart David Dickinson*

## POET'S PROBLEM

He sat in the study trying to think,
Looking out on the garden, searching for
Inspiration, now and then putting ink
On the paper, straggling black marks. The more
He wrote, the less sense it made, and in vain
He searched for new words that wouldn't come.
He knew what to write, looking up at the lane
Pictured on the wall: looking for the key
To the way to set his thoughts down on paper.
Yet it evaded him. He thought about
Giving up: going away, having a
Rest. However, he kept at it, staring out
Into space. Ideas, confused. He wished . . .
He thought more and soon the poem was finished.

*James Adlam*

## REVENGE

We come from dust - then back we go
Sometime - somewhere - somehow we know.
For me - I'd rather not lie still
I think - I'd like to move about
My ashes scattered to the winds
Perhaps - to help a flower grow.
But then - I can remember well
The ones who tried to do me wrong
No need for me to call their name
They know it like a haunting song.
So if one day they're stepping out
Strolling down the street
A wind blows up - whistling about
And knocks them off their feet.
There rolled around upon the ground
And then - they feel the pain
The burning - stinging - in their eye
Can drive them quite insane.
It can't be dirt - he gave a cry
I'm sure it is a bee.
Think hard - my friend
Think back - again
It could -
And might be -
      me.

*Frank Serafino Fontana*

# NO WORK TOMORROW

The coal black collier stood there
His face was ravaged with sorrow
And the tears rolled down his cheeks
He had just finished his last shift
There would be no work for him tomorrow
No more no more would he dig the coal
That was more than just a way of life
Not just a job but a labour of love
Digging in the dark as the sun shone above
He stood as if he was a slab of coal
As he watched the cage bring the men to the top
Then he bowed his head and sobbed
As the pit wheel came slowly to a stop
Slowly now the men went home
All joined together in one last song
As night time came and snow fell hard
The collier still stood there
His tears turned to ice upon his face
As the light went from his eyes
They found him frozen there at dawn
His dead eyes still filled with sorrow
All his working life he had given his best
In the cemetery that overlooked the mine
They gently laid the collier to rest
Better this than no work at all
He couldn't live without his mine
And the thought of no work tomorrow.

*Christine Isaac*

## HEALING

When the dead-black skulks
Enshrouding me
Smothering screams
Stifling touch with reality
When the lost being inside my skull shrieks in pain of hope distorted
Sense changing faces of moon at watch.

I might rather drown than struggle and strain for breath and light
But then your golden healing
Energy in fingertips molten-smooth
Balm to the shadowed spirit
Sending light to shimmer silken on my skin
Caress, soothing, free
Dark side open unveiled.

*Maggie Ayres*

## LIGHTHOUSE KEEPER

The lighthouse keeper his
Name was Tam
Over the seas his eyes did
Scan

Looking for vessels that
Had blown off course
through the wind and rain
At hurricane force

Seamen looked for that
Beacon of light
In treacherous conditions
On a stormy night

To carry them home on
The crest of a wave
And not be dragged to a
Watery grave.

*Marilyn Davidson*

## THE JOKE'S ON ME

To me life's a joke
to enjoy what I can
I don't mean to offend
but it seems I always am.
I open my mouth
and say what I think
but always end up
stirring up a big stink
I go to the pub
to have a good time
but on every occasion
leave my brain behind
You say I talk over you
and practically ignore you
I shout you down
but in reality adore you
I just can't find the words
to express what I feel
it's my biggest downfall I know
but I just can't see
the hurt that I cause
the pain that you have
to me deep inside
it makes me so sad
to finish my thoughts
I look up above
and pray to my Lord
not to let me lose your love
I don't want you to leave
and wish I could say
what I feel deep inside
to make you stay
Sorry!

*Graham Nairn*

## WHY ME?

'I am a divorced child,' said the boy,
Mum and Dad don't live together anymore.
Was it my fault
they shouted and argued all the time?

If I was 'specially good, I thought at first, then maybe, just
maybe, we would all be a family again,
Other times I felt confused, sad and angry with everyone
Now I have a step-father and Dad has a new girlfriend.

Split down the middle, that's how it feels,
Torn apart like a discarded family photograph,
New brother, new sister, childminder after school,
I suppose they're okay, but life can be a drag!

Two homes, new families,
Some nights I wake up and wonder where I am
I am not really confused, least not about who I am
But oh I do miss my gran, I think she'd understand.

Two sets of toys, more time for treats,
Mum and Dad still argue, but not so bad
Playing computer games, football training too,
Making new friends, now that can be cool!

'Mu-u-m,' 'What's for tea?'

*Dorothy Wilson*

## THE NEW PASTOR

Our new pastor oh Lord,
what a difference he's made,
the people are coming wanting
to be saved.
An inspiration he is, for us all to see,
his ideas and plans, please God,
let them be.

*Doreen Davies*

## GONE TO SEED

Returned, now the fields are parched.
With cows gone
the stubbled grass, short-cropped straw,
the vestige of their homemaking.

Purpled thistles
rise triumphant 'til they're mown,
ready for the next fattening.
Make hay while you can.

The lake hums as flies buzz
and silent butterflies visit
the swarming weeds that
the reeds hopelessly wave away.

Gone to seed,
the land is ravaged
no time to know its ways.
Footpaths melt beneath the
bramble march.
The echo of the footfall fades.

*Rebecca Sandover*

## HAGHILL CLASSROOM

Haghill classroom, four-square grim,
November fog cold creeping in;
Four bare bulbs vain fight the dim
And on the classroom floor
An Islay lass hears not Glasgow grim
But her own dear Islay shore.

She sings strange words I do not know
But somehow, her hearts feelings flow
Straight to my heart, make me know
What ne'er I'd known before:
The silver sand and strong sea-tow
That sweeps around Ardmore.

We learn the song in English. Sing
Words not drawn from an island spring
And tho' they be but poor, they bring
A semblance of her yearning.
O'er sixty years can still me wing
To that moment of my learning.

*Andrew Douglas*

## POPPY FIELDS

The poppy fields which yield
many undug graves,
and upon these fallen hero's lie
a single poppy which gave
peace and hope to many men,
who stuck in craters of the bomb
the colours of the poppy sing out its peaceful song.
The hand of God comes down
and takes up all of thy,
the hero's who have passed away
God takes you to the sky.
All the living in their grief
who weep both night and day,
remember their beloved on that day so grey,
and all the poppies in the fields,
sway in grief and cry.
The trenches and the fields are silenced
for those men who did bravely die.

*Tom Lee  (12)*

## FOR ALL MANKIND

Earth, who hears you weep
From the pain and destruction that man has inflicted,
In both thought word and deed
Your tears, his greed.

Some listen to your cry for help
But too few are they for your oceans of sadness.
Ridiculed for their compassion by the powerful,
Also few, controlling the thoughts of many.

So, child of the universe, open your mind
Your world begs wisdom,
That born of love from within your heart
To regain dignity, peace and balance for all mankind.

*Beverley Latter*

# I Know Now . . .

I know now what it felt like when the sun
sent first his radiance over sleeping earth
To say 'Awake, awake! Day has begun'
And earth stirred from forgetfulness to mirth,
As birds in song carolled the early hours.
And lambs and all young things gambolled in play.
Soft fleecy clouds began their race, and flowers
opened their golden eyes to greet the day.
All nature echoed with the sweet refrain
And ancient trees, in whom the sap moved slow,
Rustled their leaves in whispers, young again
In all the morning's glory; this I know!
And now I walk on stars because you smiled:
Head in the clouds, and heart with song beguiled.

*Eric Ferguson*

## IMPRESSIONS OF CHURCH

This place of ultimate tranquillity,
At once restoring one's sanity.
The welcome creak of wooden pews,
Taking away those dreadful blues.

The simple beauty of the altar cloth,
The muffled echo of someone's cough.
The hymn books waiting at the door
Yes, this is what our voices are for.

The gentle flicker of the Easter candle
Giving an atmosphere too serene to handle.
The sacred organ's majestic tone
Reaching inside, easing every bone.

The smell of incense, fragrant and pure.
The ills of the world now have a cure.
The congregation stands, the procession begins,
Watched over by angels with golden wings.

Here in God's house we offer our praise,
Knowing he's here, now and always.
That perfect atonement of God's only son,
The battle to be fought, already won.

*John Bills*

## PHANTOM RULER STRIKES AGAIN

The trends invisible machine, that makes the rules,
that everyone thinks they have to obey.
To be accepted as normal we have to become abnormal,
Defying our own instincts and desires.
The image we hold of normality is a mere phantom.
A phantom chased by the multitudes,
But can never be realised because it does not exist.
If only it could be killed!
But how can one kill that which belongs to imagination
And so, we are entrapped in a vision of normality,
Prisoners, one and all.

*Teresa McDonough*

## WAITING FOR SOMETHING MORE

Dark is the day dark is the night
Out of my mind out of your sight
To live with or to live without
Buried alive with mistrust and doubt

Sitting alone in the back of my mind
Wanting to see but I'd rather be blind
Lost, not looking, or just can't find
Innocent childhood left far behind

Hoping and waiting hiding afraid
Picking up promises already made
Discarding dreams that are already dead
Lost in confusion inside my head

*Isabel Muir*

# HEAT

From high in the sky
To the depths of the earth
Heat that we know
Can be friend - even foe.
Over great barren lands
It leaves deserts of sand
Life it will give
That we may all live.
From tropical forests
Flowers that bloom
Chickens that hatch
Not a moment too soon.
Hearts all aglow from fires burning bright
This heat that we know gives us our daily light.

*Sheila Johnson*

# THE POINT OF WARS

The point of wars I do not see,
It's swelling up inside of me.
Why can't we just let others be,
To their own satisfaction?

Having wars against your own will,
The gaps that these men have to fill.
Brothers, sons, and fathers killed,
In wars leading to nowhere.

Civil wars are still a disgrace,
Religions blow up in your face.
Saying prayers and saying your grace,
May not get you much further.

God wouldn't like you to have wars,
Breaking a lot of country's laws.
Killing for God would only cause
His disrespect and sadness.

So next time you say wars are 'Cool,'
Remember who may be to fall.
Yourself, your neighbour, we're all fuel.
To be lost to mighty wars.

*Lara Marshall (11)*

## A NEW-BORN'S THOUGHTS

I entered this world and into the light
From a place that was warm, but dark as night.
I felt a sharp pain, I knew not why.
From where had it come? I started to cry.
I was laid down on my mother's breast,
I felt at peace and wanted to rest
I started my journey from far, far away
But I'd arrived at last and wanted to stay.

*M S Maldon*

## THIS WORLD

My dreams scattered
My life doesn't matter
Poverty and war
Comes knocking on our door

People with riches
People in ditches
Working all day
Without enough pay

The rich and the posh
Throw away dosh
While some people starve
No gravestones to carve.

*Heather Millichap*

# COUNTDOWN TO MILLENNIUM

The ticking and clicking are on the wall
Recording the daily digital score,
The days, the hours, the minutes, the seconds,
Waiting for that day to be reckoned.

They're waiting and dreaming and planning and scheming
They've even built a mighty great dome.
But will they remember when it gets to December
The place for the heart is the home?

Christ was departed and AD got started
Clocking the months and the years,
As the grains slip away into night, into day,
2000 seems long in our ears.

In 999 did they calendar time?
Did they count out the year in reverse?
Did they sing Christmas carols? Exchange bows and arrows?
Did they see treble '0' as a curse?

And are we cursed by wars and much worse?
Famine, flood and invention,
Are we servants to some and masters of none?
But maybe that's the intention.

So the pendulum groans and the metronome moans
And the sands of time wait for no man,
We can't pack away the night and the day
Or stop clocks like W H Auden.

But if Kipling's minute we put something in it
For everyone's good it would be,
When the counting's done down to number one.
Well, we'll just have to wait and see.

*Mary A Atkinson*

# A POEM FOR PAUL ASTON -
*(On His 11<sup>th</sup> Birthday)*

Now look here Paul, you know the rules
You mustn't handle dangerous tools;
That saw you've got is a top class brand
But, one silly slip and you've damaged your hand.

Just wait until you're as old as me
Before you start to live dangerously;
Apply some restraint through the passing years
And you'll save yourself oceans of sadness and tears.

Whatever the structure I wish to erect
I always treat saws with the greatest respect;
Especially the circular ones with motor attached
Why, the care I display could hardly be matched.

I've learned my lessons when using tools
Too sharp to grace the hands of fools;
This advice then I pass to you
Just wait until you are forty-two.

Now look here Dad, I'm eleven now,
And conscious of my intelligent brow.
Bright of brain and fleet of foot
Sharp-eyed as the hawk to boot.

Remember that it was last night
You gave yourself an awful fright:
With circular saw, heard rotating still,
You put it on the window sill.

Oh! The language as it fell
And nearly gashed your toes as well
As marking marks where they shouldn't be
And yet you're so concerned for me.

Now look here Paul, cut out the chatter
And concentrate on a practical matter
With a lot less talk and a little more do:
Hold the end of this plank whilst I saw it through.

*Grandpa Aston, October 1997*

**Jack Aston**

# WHERE IGNORANCE IS BLISS

A young lady was driving home
in her new motor car,
She just had passed her driving rest
and things went well, so far.

The road was rather narrow
it really was not broad,
A great truck in front of her
was shedding out its load.

She had to tell the driver
or someone else instead,
The truck would soon be empty
the load would soon be shed.

She blew her horn and shouted out
and soon he called a halt.
She said 'Your load is pouring out
and I think it is salt.'

He smiled at her and then he said,
'Now you are a halfwit,
I'm working for the town, my dear,
and pouring out the grit.'

**Alistair Grewar**

## THE DAFFODIL

I love the golden daffodil
Each year I wait for spring
To see them in their glory
In parks and meadows
Even on the roadside.

They hold their head so proudly
It gives us quite a lift
And fills our hearts with gladness
To know that spring is here

***Joan & Sarah Gwilliam***

## WAVES

I have dreamed this place into reality,
Sea, sky-blue. Sky, sea-green.
White spray crashing against ancient rocks, playing
Hide and seek with the sun.

And she, polo sweater tight against her body
Moves, long black hair tossing.
Tiny feet in multicoloured Doc Martens,
Legs long, black flares, clinging.

I watch, entranced, this child of mine, sand, sea and she
Laughing, singing, dancing.
As the waves, towards womanhood. I should feel warm
But I am cold. Ice-blue.

*Sheila Crawley*

## NEIGHBOURS

I have a special neighbour who is nearly ninety-three
(We live in sheltered flats and we're as cosy as can be)
She has a hearing problem and she can barely see,
But she loves to have a visitor who will help to pour the tea.

At times her memory lapses and often she will say
'Is it Saturday - or Sunday' - or 'Who's coming here today?'
'Is it the one who does my feet, or the one who does my hair?'
And I know I'll find her windows wide as she really loves fresh air.

Round and round the passageways she takes her daily walks
And meets with other residents to enjoy their little talks.
She is a brave and plucky lady, as anyone can see,
And though she thinks I'm good to her - I know she's good for me.

*Annie Starkey*

## A GIFT OF LOVE

Children are a gift of love.
A symbol of parents' devotion.
They make our lives complete
And give us motivation
To strive for a better world for them,
To live in peace and joy.
This is the wish of all of us
For every girl and boy.

*Norma Pepper*

## CHRISTMAS

Christmas is a time of joy,
There is a new baby boy.
Three wise kings with gifts so rich
Come to the stable guided by a star.

Children are so happy
Santa has come to them
With presents galore
Christmas dinner -
Yum! Yum! Yum!

Outside the snow is falling
Red berries fill the hedges.
Carol singers are singing -
This is Christmas time.

*James Canning*

## AMY

She starts her day with cries of 'Dad,'
She tells him of the dreams she's had.
Next down the stairs she wants to go,
Hurry Mam, you go too slow.
From room to room she runs around
'Til brother and sister she has found.
Her plan right now, and for the day
Are for them to choose which games to play.

The day for her has gone too fast
But for brother and sister - a rest at last,
'It's time to bath now,' Mam has said
Then Dad will take her off to bed.
He gently lays her down to sleep
Reminding her, her dreams to keep
So when she wakes and calls out 'Dad.'
She can tell him of the dreams she's had.

*Linda Jenkins*

# HALLOWE'EN

Hallowe'en is a frightening night
The witches on their broomsticks going the speed of light,
Zombies rise from the dead,
All the children hiding in their bed.

The witches on their broomsticks
All night long,
Whistling through the darkness
Singing a terrible song.

Tonight you hurry and run,
To look as best as a fiend
Because you can dress up as anything,
Because tonight is *Hallowe'en.*

**Tomas Malone**

## WITCHES

Witches flying in the sky
Look up they're flying so high.
Landing, landing, down, down, down
On the ground.
Hubble, bubble on the double
Fire burn and cauldron bubble.
Can you hear the witches
Laughing in their kitchens?
*Ghosts*
Scary, spooky ghosts
Floating around the lamp posts
shouting *'Boo!'*
Flighty, mighty ghosts
Creeping through the keyholes
Chanting
'I'm going to get you!'

**Ciara Delaney**

# HALLOWE'EN

Hallowe'en is here at last,
There's the fireworks,
Hear the blast.

Ghosts are calling,
Night is falling
Here the witches cackle.

Devils are coming out of hell,
Witches are cooking up a spell.
Dead are coming out of their graves,
We all have to be very brave.

The witches are flying out tonight,
Hoping to give a really good fright
The little black cat sitting on the back,
Hiding in the witch's tall black hat.

***Eimear Kennedy & Orla Savage***

## CAMARADERIE - OR IN A LIBRARY TEA SHOP

Venture to the library any day you choose
enter our own Camelot give ear to other views,
poetry, music, architecture, royals, or bour geoisie,
With Vince, Dennis, Glen, Paul, Fred, Diane, and Me.

Two coffees and an apple juice, and four of toast please Rose,
our legendary table will keep you on your toes,
while we discuss the properties of ginseng, wine, or tea,
Vince, Dennis, Glen, Paul, Fred, Diane and Me.

Oh what shall we call ourselves, how shall we be known?
The Arthurians, The Brains' Trust, Intellectual Tone,
It's really most important how we're perceived to be
Vince, Dennis, Glen, Paul, Fred, Diane, and Me.

What diversity of ages, whims and interests,
no topic is taboo, no opinion depressed,
at times we beg to differ, most deferentially,
Vince, Dennis, Glen, Paul, Fred, Diane, and Me.

Oh how we shall miss our times of pure high art,
as singly we're called for new pastures to depart,
rare bonds of true friendship, such camaraderie,
With Vince, Dennis, Glen, Paul, Fred, Diane, and Me.

Oft times when I slumber, and see with dream-glazed eyes
my friends at our table, my spirits seems to rise
to new-found dimensions, to worlds as yet to be,
with Ben, Wolfgang, Franz, Ralph, John Betjeman, and me.

*John Clark*

## EASTER AHEAD

Easter bonnets happy faces,
Chiffon net and feathers bright,
Flowers ribbons bows and laces,
Make the spring a welcome sight.

Some bonnets large as planets placed,
On each fashionable head,
Lilac green with yellow traced,
Like a coloured rainbow spread.

Worn in friendly competition,
To celebrate the time of spring,
Easter new life old tradition,
That's what Easter bonnets bring.

Spring is a time for new beginnings,
Chicks and bunnies go to heads,
Easter bonnets with their trimmings,
Rival the bright flower-beds.

All of nature wears a garment,
Pleasing to the eye in spring,
Fun and fashion main intent,
Celebrate the joys they bring.

Pleasure of colour to the eye,
Pleasure through design and style,
Fashion's parade goes quickly by,
Why not watch it with a smile.

***Kathleen Mary Scatchard***

## SOMETIMES

Sometimes you drive me crazy
    mad as mad can be.
Sometimes I wish I didn't love you so
    until I remember
 - You probably think the same about me.

On the bad days
when we're not getting on.
Sometimes I wish I didn't love you so
    until I remember
 - It's not always you, in the wrong.

All in all to sum up
    our joint life (like any others) has its ups and downs.
Sometimes I wish I didn't love you so
    until I remember
 - That to live with me isn't always easy, at all.

***C A Bond***

## WELCOME POSTMARK
*(A Haiku)*

I still get a stir
When I see your envelope
Brown on the doormat.

It is a great thrill
To see the 'Forward' postmark
'Wainman Road, Woodston.

Please don't change the style
It gives such pleasure to poets
To see it arrive -

What can be in there?
An acceptance can it be?
A copy returned?

Can you understand
The pleasure your letter brings
To budding writers?

***Richard Stoker***

# HAIKUS

Tiny bell swaying
the first of nature's criers
ringing in the spring.

Invisible imp
sliding silently through the night
and darkening grass.

Silent visitor
making miniature hillocks
and disrupting life.

Ferocious devil
whiptailing mountainous water
and reaping havoc.

Ariel ballet
playing on teasing winds
spread a white mantle.

Baleful gloomy light
from a moth-eaten blackness
casts weird shadows.

Brilliant coloured arch
dancing across the heavens
after summer rain.

Exploding fireball
shoots golden rays over hilltops
and caresses trees.

*Brian Stewart*

## DIFFERENT DREAMS

I thought a lover was someone to trust,
Someone who wouldn't run out on me.
How wrong I was, how easily mislead.
How gullible, how naive could I be?

To place my trust in one I loved,
In a man I thought was mine.
A man who I believed would be with me,
On the last day we saw the sun shine.

It's hard, now, to accept he's with another,
A woman I've never met, have never wanted to,
But who has won a battle I never knew I was fighting,
That I would have fought if I knew I needed to.

The betrayal of trust, of the gift of my heart,
Hurts far deeper than I knew it could.
It's fallen into depths I never knew existed,
Never, ever dreamed I would.

I see two lovers holding hands,
I swap faces, yours and mine.
Am I wrong to want you back?
To spend my life in sorrow, to pine?

The years we spent together, the hours,
I shall never forget, I can't, even if I wanted to,
You were a part of my life, I thought I was part of yours,
Instead I'm left with regrets, not the same as you.

I can't believe you can move on so quickly,
Can live the future, forget the past.
The past that mattered so much to me,
That I thought was there to last.

*Patricia Cunningham*

## BALMY DAYS OF SPRING
*(Dedicated to Maureen)*

The winter coolness still lingered
As I strolled the woods today
Noisy woodpeckers chipping away high above
Birds making a most harmonious din
Lest we forget 'twas spring
Everywhere so wonderfully bright
Violet, primrose, celandine, woodbine too
Even bluebells pushing through
Soon to blend their hue
The carpet of gold is a sight to behold
With the sun filtering in through unfurled trees
Just a hint of a breeze
Mysterious shadows abound, obscure pathways
Now to be found, a gentle thud upon the ground
A muntjac too shy to stay around
Rabbits scampering, some in fright,
Some stop to give a curious stare
I want to share the joy of it
So intense is my delight

***Barbara Ling***

## WINTER SHOCK

Dawn blush - rose pink,
Winter robin - in the sink,
Night sky - turned blue,
Another day - something new,
In the glow - sun fading!
Dense cloud - east approaching,
Hills grey - then whitening,
Red clouds - sun appearing,
Golden light - intensifying,
Silver larch - silhouetting,
Snowflakes - gently falling,
Scraping car - cold appalling!
Icicles - on the railing,
Postman's breath - visibly steaming,
Revelry - head splitting!
Deep snow - wheels spinning,
Radio - more coming!

*Tom Ritchie*

## AN EVENING SKY

A boiling red sky falls
In a strobe motion,
Into a deep grey haze
Above me.

The birds give up
Their sweet song,
As darkness chokes them
In its numbing embrace.

While all else fades,
Memory hangs still
Like a blade
Over my wrists.

***Krystian Taylor***

## DIFFERENT COLOUR

Black, white, dark, light,
Afraid of the day, feared of the night,
Groups on corners stand,
Sticks and weapons held in their hands,
Fear, hate, nerves grate,
Heads turning, watching, listening,
Sharp steel in lamplight glistening,
Running feet on pavement tapping,
Breath in exhaust, chests rasping,
Reach home safe now . . . no.
Bullet from guns already let go.
People gather anger within.
All this bloodshed for the colour of their skin,
Mandela won but has peace come
Or undercover of a badge the slaying still goes on.
This land was theirs before they were made
To grovel in dirt and renamed slaves

*Winifred Wardle*

# UNDER TRANSVAAL SKIES

The breezes changed colour
Casting out white blight,
Dismissing township blues,
Red menace was just a ruse
To delay,
The long walk to *freedom*.

While everyone tries,
To work out,
What the word means.

*Amandla! . . . Ngawethu!*

After Mandela,
Others will come . . .

**Steve Taylor**

# THE VOICE OF FREEDOM

See the boundary fences fall,
  Break down the segregating wall,
    Hear the trumpets' clarion call,
      The voice of freedom cries.

Release the harsh restraining chain,
  Unlock the manacles of pain,
    Let every man shout out his name,
      The voice of freedom cries.

Hear each man speak, it is his right,
  Whatever colour, black or white,
    Walk from the darkness into light,
      The voice of freedom cries.

Be not afraid to say, 'I'm me,
  It is my right, it's what I'll be,
    And I will live a life that's free'
      The voice of freedom cries.

Bands of repression, now untied,
  Angry oppression, now decried,
    Force and aggression, now denied,
      The voice of freedom cries.

Ten thousand thousand voices sing,
  Of all the joys freedom can bring,
    Apartheid - no more suffering?
      The voice of freedom cries!

*James W Sargant*

# THE ENDING OF TYRANNY

It's now the end of Apartheid.
Time to live in peace.
Have we found the solution?
Will the enmity decrease?

The end of racial segregation.
Tyranny, poverty, hate and distrust.
Goodbye to lies, discrimination.
Bury the past, let it turn to dust.

Time to push for human rights.
Reinforce our belief in the solution,
Sharing, caring and setting our sights
On bringing its end to fruition.

Let's hope we have learned to survive.
Whatever our colour or creed.
Let the black and white learn to live,
Without rancour malice or greed.

*J McGill*

## SOUTH AFRICAN DREAM

A cauldron on a white
Fire of hate,
The blacks accursed plight
Doomed to wait,
Turned history ash grey
Though to come,
Recondite hid the day
Loathed by some
A time to wash the shame -
Apartheid -
That controversial name
Known worldwide,
Away for evermore.
Protest grew,
A kind of racial war,
Till anew
Burst forth the victims' rights;
'Let us learn
Together, blacks and whites;
Do not burn
Our fundamental dues!'
Wild the plea,
Then , at long last, the news,
Blacks were free;
Dissension in some hearts
Cankers on
But, hush, a new age starts,
Evil gone.
Come true, part of God's scheme
The great apartheid dream.

*Ruth Daviat*

## AFRIKAANER APPREHENSION

Mandela's rainbow country.
Revelation - revolution,
Will it still remain a homeland for me?
For the colours in the rainbow
Are uneven in their bands,
Can there be even distribution of the land?
Our people once more laager
To protect what they have won,
Now after many generations
Will we lose our own?
Do rainbow colours mingle?
Blacks, Malays and Coloureds rarely mix.
Boer Afrikaaners and other Europeans,
Could we agree this mingling
Proud of our pure stock?
For now the rainbow is a shimmer,
Shining through tumbling storm clouds -
Offering a promise the turmoil soon will end.
But if we will attain this
We must tear down ancient fences
Of prejudice and colour and social expectation.
A pot of change is bubbling
We're all ingredients in it . . .
In my beloved South Africa
I pray I may remain.

*Di Bagshawe*

## THE COOKING POT

Two sides, one black the other white,
Two laws, one wrong the other right.
Set one is free to rule, to live and fly,
Set two hemmed in, crushed left to die.

Someone lifted off the lid for all to see,
There was one law for them another for thee.
These things they really did not like,
So they stirred the pot and started a fight.

It took some time for things to simmer down,
But now there is enough freedom to go around,
Leaving each one a bowl that is full,
Giving them room to live and to grow.

*Pauline Uprichard*

## SOUTH AFRICA

A time of historic importance,
The day awaited long,
For in discarding apartheid
Came new symbolic song.

With this acknowledged union
Each thought's salient now,
Their votes chose Nelson Mandela
To take President's vow.

This man, unfairly imprisoned
For long confining years,
Kept faith he'd somehow legislate
To dry a Nation's tears.

A place of tremendous potential
With dreams blossoming truth,
Their hopes suddenly realised,
Their views redeeming youth.

We pray for continued harmony,
That long dissensions cease,
That this momentous occasion
Brings South Africa *peace.*

*Eileen Shenton*

## ANIMAL RIGHTS

The creature sits,
Both deaf and blind,
Caged, not moving.
Man tries to find,
Some newer lipstick
Or new perfume,
That will not damage
A lady's bloom,
Her painted lips
To tempt some man
Have slowly shortened
The creature's span.
The rabbit should be
Left to roam
A burrow not
A cage its home 25.1.99

*Jean Turner*

## ANIMAL KINGDOM

When God made the world before he ever made you and me,
He made the birds that fly in the air, the fish that swim in the sea,
The lions and the tigers that roam the jungle forest
He made all these just for us;

But man has abused his creation and taken liberties
Inflicting painful tests upon helpless animals to save humanity,
With make-up trials for vanity, drugs so we won't sue,
They are even killed for sport and rounded up for zoos;

They have every right, as we do, to live in peace and harmony
But now they do not trust us we keep them under lock and key,
We shouldn't abuse God's creation for testing or for sport
I think animal testing should be banned and the culprits
                                    brought to court!

*Julie McKenzie*

## LIFE'S CRUELTY

No one cares anymore
behind the laboratory doors,
scared and lonely waiting
for tests,
they're just animals of creation
so why put them to a test,
you always think you know best,
God knows what's best, that's love
not bloody tests.

***Sharon Laurie***

# TOM

I am a cat,
Small, male, black and white.
I have no name
Though Mum called me Tom.
I miss my Mum.

I live in a pen
With lots more cats;
The food's not good,
Hygiene poor, pen smells.
I miss my Mum.

I hear the dread words
'Tests' and 'operation'.
Men stick sharp things in me,
They frighten me.
I miss my Mum.

Sometimes I hear mentioned
A place called 'home';
It sounds nice - maybe
I'll go there some day.
I miss my Mum.

There's noises outside,
Shouts like 'Close down';
People are fighting
Which frightens me too.
I miss my Mum.

They have come for me -
I am so frightened -
What will they do to me?
There's no escape -
Mum, Mum, where are you?

***Maria-Christina***

## THE PLIGHT OF ANIMALS

Imagine if us humans in the next life were changed
Into some animal restricted by chains
Thrust into cages, crowded prison labs
Held down, against will, bisected on a slab

Such cruelty we would never allow on ourselves
Yet animals scream out from the laboratory shelves
Extreme suffering should never be forced upon
Any living creature of which we belong

They are all God's creatures, deserving of this earth
Vulnerable and helpless, no respect of animals worth
Animals no voice, we must speak on their behalf
To change human views into saving animal lives.

*R E Humphrey*

## BAN ON TESTING

We throw up our hands in horror,
   say 'This testing must not be,
the cruelty, the suffering
   on a creature, oh, so wee.'
But - if we stop to think awhile
   what else is there to do?
Would you rather *mother* suffered
   because they could not test what's new?
And if you should lose your dear ones
   because new drugs could not be tested -
would you hold *then* to strict ideals,
   weeping for a young life wasted?
Using animals for cosmetics
   I think is wholly wrong -
I only hope a ban on this
   will shortly come along.
But, when it comes to *human* lives
   the matter's complicated -
how *can* you weigh your mother's life -
   without these trials she would be dead!
As yet, there are no other ways
   to test the safety of these drugs,
we *must* do that to stop disease
   and eradicate life-threatening bugs.
We hope and pray the time will come
   when more civilised means are used -
until then, I'm sad to say,
   these animals will be abused.

*Joyce Hockley*

## LIVE AND LET LIVE

Dogs, cats and many of God's creatures
In scientific experiments they have featured
But now at last
That is all over
Let's hope that they can live in clover
Children's pets
Adults' friends
See if the means defeats the ends
The cruelty that they had
The thought it makes me very sad
It's time for change
Time to mend
Now thankfully
This is the end

*Jeffrey Shedlow*

## AND ALL FOR WHAT?

Face of beauty, so you say
Eyes that sparkle going astray
Lips so full, so flavoured, sweet, so voluptuous, in a voluminous way
And all for what?
A fuller, more happier, complete life, that's all you can say
Who had to suffer and suffered humanely and died
Pause for thought. Think!
And all for what?

Body of a goddess
Breasts polygon pyramids, propped prongs
Legs so long, you think, firm steel, soft as silk, streamline like a pyralid
And all for what?
Because you want to look refine, parading golden sandy beaches
Why is it some poor, numb, innocence creatures have to die?
You took their life!
And all for that!

How does it feel to look beautiful, wonderful, chic, divine
From your lips and breasts their life blood cry out
All the time!

Before you make up your mind
To be what you were never born to be
Think twice. Act wise
You are saving a helpless, innocence life

And is it not better to search for grace and beauty from within
Greater is human loveliness kindled through love its known
From its inner fire, other exquisiteness, excellence of human
                                        nature flow
And at the end you'll feel so much better, knowing all you have,
Is not someone else's bits and pieces made up from spare parts

*Rosetta Stone*

# FACE VALUES

The mascara ran at the moment you cried
This product was cheap, but an animal died
Your lipstick looks nice, is it called a 'Blood Red'?
I wonder because there's an animal dead
Your cheeks look quite flushed with the blusher you wear
An animal suffered but who gives a care
Your eye shadow colours your lids pastel blue
An animal bled just to beautify you
Caged and abused just for vanity's sake
Tested and tortured for men on the make
Cosmetics to pamper and pretty your face
Forgetting the pain and the total disgrace
If there has to be tests for a human's welfare
Why not test on a human who hasn't a prayer
A murderer serving a sentence for life
Would at least serve a purpose if under a knife
Why suffer poor animals without a choice
They would campaign themselves
If they'd only a voice!

*David Whitney*

# PREY

Patiently watchful
Silently skulking forward
Fatally alert

Sudden disturbance
Prey fluttering scattering
Panic confusion

Feathers a-flying
Flustered squawking and shrieking
Then silence surrounds

*Elaine Buck*

# BACK TO SCHOOL, 1998

Six years ago, my daughter gave me a grandson!
A precious gift, a prize with no winning
And, although I'm in my twilight years,
Life rejuvenates in his beginnings!

In 1998, I went back to primary school,
At tables, not neat rows, I sat,
I found the ABC lived in Letterland,
Annie Apple, Bouncy Ben, Clever Cat!

I discovered the National Cirrculum,
Numeracy, not sums, and the Literacy Hour,
Surfing, not on boards, but the Internet,
Found computers are the ones in power!

His fifth birthday was a real celebration,
Nothing as mundane as a party you see,
A visit with ten to a fun ball pool,
Next, chicken nuggets at McDonald's for tea.

Next year, I look forward to new hobbies,
Thinking back to my pianoforte and such,
Karate and drama have been mentioned,
I really won't get out of touch!

The future is full of new beginnings,
Secondary school, university, who knows?
Followed by a career and then marriage,
My happiness knows no bounds, does it show?

Through this little boy life is starting anew,
He's guiding me past the millennium,
God has turned my sunset into a new dawn,
I've thrown out cares and stifling tedium!

*Pat Heppel*

## 15 JANUARY 1998

The tiny baby reached out her hand
And the earth knew all that she would do
And be in spite of all the misery.

I turned away in sadness
At this cruel world's madness
And for my own part feel no gladness
Or hope within my heart.

*Pauline Scragg*

# LEGACY

After you'd gone and I'd got my head together,
Slowly learned to live alone
Without your brooding presence,
I dreamed one night of things you'd left behind.
I saw them clearly
As I woke into that dream.
A velvet, half-grown panther,
Watchful, sleek and menacing;
A silly puppy dog, that fawned
And slobbered round my skirts -
But worst of all,
A moth-eaten hyena,
Snapping and snarling at my legs
As I tried to ring the council man
To take them all away.

*Jean Oxley*

## DEPARTURES AND ARRIVALS

Departure of hope, departure of scope,
Arrival at conviction I'm the world's biggest dope;

Departure of goal and destination,
Arrival at 'black hole' of desperation;

Departure of sense of being required,
Arrival of omnipresent prospect of 'being fired';

Departure of enjoyment of what I once liked most,
Arrival of lethargy, forlornly, having 'given up ghost';

Departure of hope for being a 'real man',
Arrival, instead, at embarrassing sham;

Departure of sense of self-respect,
Arrival, unavoidably, at self-neglect;

Departure in respect of more favoured rival,
Arrival at double-edged sword instinctive survival;

Departure from being noticed for being sedate and nice,
Arrival at temptation by all that is base and vice;

Departure needing to enjoy a thing returned to,
Arrival of doubt about where, the how and the who . . .

Departure from having no time for things worthwhile to do,
Arrival at having the time but no money or clue what to do;

Departure from one closed door,
Arrival at more.

Departure not liking the way things appear to be going,
Arrival of fearing 'self-flagulation' I thereby am showing;

Departure from lack of belief in ever finding 'the key',
Arrival at exorcism by writing - to see what we might see . . .

Departure from one plane of reality in life,
Arrival at oblique counterbalance to bemoanings and strife;

Departure, at last, from having no usefulness at all -
Arrival at recognition of use - no matter how small!

***Paul Bartlett***

## GOLDEN OPPORTUNITY

After I was widowed I turned a new page.
I plucked up courage and joined *The College of Third Age.*
Sitting at home getting depressed was not my goal
but to keep my brain alert, extend my knowledge, and refresh my soul!

We can choose all sorts of subjects from various classes;
sharing same age group and interest, time quickly passes.
In relaxed atmosphere we enjoy this leisure,
gain new contact, confidence and lots of pleasure!

It is so easy to drift into a *low* when on your own.
Be grateful to be alive, and don't moan!
Take advantage of the *golden opportunity*
show intentions and be part of the community!
Exercise your talent and creation!

Achievement and to *belong* is better than any medication!

*Annemarie Poole*

## HOPING FOR A BETTER YEAR!

The year known as nineteen ninety and eight,
is the year my clan will forever hate.
Two children who'd moved out came back again,
my arthritis flared up, I was wracked with pain.

Then my husband, an older, kindly bloke,
surprised us all by having a mild stroke.
Late October, things had settled a bit,
husband's birthday, went to Paris for a trip.

Let's leave behind last years worries and cares,
as nineteen ninety eight was a nightmare.
A daughter's decided to get married,
hope this year by happiness we'll be carried.

*Susan Mullinger*

# CALL TO ARMS

Across the road I watched them go,
those raw recruits to meet the foe.
Some teenage lads - a motley crowd
Mothers stood silent, with heads bowed.

When duty called they weren't afraid
to offer themselves, while women prayed.
Their safe return; on bended knee,
the unknown future - none could see . . .

Old soldiers shook their heads in pain,
to see our youth exposed again.
To sip from cup (and taste the gall)
they too had gone - adventure's call . . .

Upright they marched with heads held high
some to live and some to die.
Those men so brave, and no-one's slave!
So cheer them on; give them a wave!

***Ivy Cawood***

# CHRISTMAS EVE 1998

On Christmas Eve 1998
someone knocked upon our door.
It was dark
and no-one had ever
knocked on our front door
on Christmas Eve before.

'Who is it?' I called
'Willi,' he replied.
'Would you kindly go round to the back door?'
then I asked him inside.

He presented me with a Christmas Card
and a beautiful flower in a pot.
Colour deep red.
Me and Winston liked it such a lot.

I was so taken back when he gave it to me
I was speechless, don't you see?

'Thank you Willi, for being so kind.
You must have many kind thoughts of us
in your mind. Thank you.'

***Amy Barrett***

# GHOST PATROL

The pastor walked the churchyard
the roll call there he read
and a thousand spirit soldiers,
returned before him from the dead.

This ghostly apparition
so sinister to see.
Stood bayonets at the ready
and all expectantly.

Upon the air came a roll of drums
and all the tall trees there suddenly hissed.
But through it all, these proud men stood tall
shrouded in the morning mist.

It was then the order was given
and they marched on as before.
But this was no normal regiment
marching into a fairy tale war.

The very sight of uniforms,
and bullets then did fly,
but the bullets went right through their target,
so no one there did die.

Back to their churchyard resting place
the soldiers then did go.
There moral was lifted higher
there enemy all laid low.

And as the mist slowly lifted
the world was a peace once more.
But how many times had they risen this way
would this continue for ever more.

Now every night at the stroke of twelve
a bugler sounds retreat.
Hoping that in future years
this will halt their marching feet.

*Victor Robert Allen Day*

# DIVIDED SOCIETIES

Equality is what is needed
in this troubled world today.
For with the division of the poor and rich
this is not a clever way.

There are people who have lots of wealth
as others struggle to survive.
This creates a troubled atmosphere
and keeps animosity alive.

If the poor were offered security
and a decent way of life.
This would banish all those acts
of terrorism and strife.

There are people whom you can't improve
that is those with no ambition.
But it is only right to try and help
to better their condition.

We are all God's people
who were made in his creation.
So we are all equal in his eyes
with none of higher station.

*Lachlan Taylor*

# COUNTRYSIDE

The rivers on the levels tinkling along,
the birds in the trees sing their sweet song.
The people on the levels come and go,
the trees in the wind blow softly to and fro,
Green fields
Blue skies
I wander round and wonder why,
the hedgehogs are in hiding,
the badgers are asleep.
I creep around softly
creep, creep, creep.
It's getting dark
I have to go home
I leave the animals all alone . . .

*Rebecca Chester  (10)*

## ONCE LONG AGO . . .

I used to go to this school
once long ago . . .
Ten to nine each morning
off to school I'd go.
I used to play on the steps
see them over there!
Maybe this is my desk
and that could be my chair
and look there's my old classroom
that one over there!
Unforgotten memories
of days without a care . . .

*Alan Green*

## THOSE SPECIAL TIMES

What do you give a grandad who has everything that he could need?
When having gone through life with all it's ups and downs, and seen
sometimes the evidence of greed.
There's been time to realise that worthwhile happiness often comes
from the success of others.
If there is a family it can be sharing the pleasures of your sisters and
your brothers.
But if not, you may have spent time with grandchildren from when
each one was a tot.
And now you can be proud of their achievements and yet reminisce -
you can still see them in the cot.
There is a limit to what we can pass on to our children, there will
be hopes and dreams.
But we must allow individuality to develop their many varied schemes.
Perhaps everyone feels at some time that sincere love, kindness and
compassion must mean contact with those that we adore.
And yet as the world becomes a relatively smaller place, separations
will be more and more.
Absence makes the heart grow fonder, but has not always consoled
when someone has been missed.
But if we can be together at special times it will be worth the wait,
if everyone is hugged and kissed.

*Reg Morris*

## A FAMILY CHRISTMAS

The shops are shut, the travelling done, it's the magic of Christmas Eve.
The night of Santa's visit, or so the children believe.

With welcoming hugs and greetings we arrive from all over the land,
linking our four generations, great family parties are planned.

Molly the cat disappears through the flap, of the influx she
doesn't approve;
Whenever the grandchildren charge into sight, it's the signal for
Madam to move.

We find our rooms and unpack our bags, the children now hopping
with glee.
As they sneakily finger the presents placed under the Christmas tree.

The house is warm, the lighting soft, decorations and greenery festive
As the adults catch up with the family news the young ones are
getting quite restive.

The table is set, we all gather round to enjoy a sociable meal,
with banter hilarious, droll teasing and jokes, repartee undertaken
with zeal.

Occasionally voices are raised, not in rage but for Great Nanny P's
chance to hear.
Amidst all the chat; much food is consumed in an atmosphere
full of good cheer.

Each one has a task preparing the fare for tomorrow's traditional roast;
then the children to bed, stockings hung, stories read, for the parents
a seasonal toast.

We sit round the fire, in friendship relaxed, discussing old times
and reflecting
on issues of interest, of hope for the world and our family
values protecting.

Chuckling Santas tread soft up the stairs, each struggling to stifle
the noise;
at the base of each bed a full stocking is placed, hopefully with
the right toys.

Together again for a hot bedtime drink as we listen for midnight
church chimes;
with enfolding love the family meets, thanking God for such
happy times.

*Ann P Price*

# REGRET

Yesterday is a hundred years away
she held the glass in hand and began to pray.
I can still taste your touch and I'm getting deeper
you thought I was sleeping but I heard every word
you cut me deep, but I'll cut deeper.
Close your eyes can you still feel me?
I've so many things to show you.
Feel my pain, taste my distaste
would you say I was wasted
when I kissed you?
Did you think I would forget?
Would you call this regret?
My eyes maybe hazy, but I can see you
I'll take it all with me
and leave you nothing.
You can take my body
because I don't need it . . .

**_Christian James Emmerson_**

# WIND

As a couple walk on a windy day
they look upon a homely house as it rains.
They find this house has an open fire
as it pours down outside.
They snuggle up together enjoying wine
and crackle.
As they look out - it's still wet
They still have to got out on their journey
so far away to meet their parents
on this cold day . . .

*Roger Brooks*

## THE POPLAR GROVE

I walk today down the poplar way,
exhilarating wind-force in my face.
Echoing in my ear, buffeting wild my hair
whipping and swishing as horses in a race.

What is it about the wind
that lifts my spirit as though one
With these poplars? Energy driven wild,
as youngsters revelling in a carnival of fun.

I walk once more among these trees, wanting
to taste the life, the strong wildness of life.
To feel its freshness in my veins,
Making me feel young again despite my years.
Oh, I so love a windy day!
Inebriating, intoxicating breath of life.
Come, breathe through me,
Enliven now these veins!

*Nora Coughlan*

## MAN'S BEST FRIEND

Man's best friend is his dog, many often say.
It's a sentiment that is so true in a most sincere way.
On the day a puppy comes into your life he ransacks your home.
How can you mind because he's so cute, you know you'll never
be alone.
Each morning his barking wakes you up when he wants to play.
Then as your feet hit the floor - whoops! He's washed them
already today.
You know you can't be cross with him when he looks to you with
his puppy eyes.
He's left a reminder in your slippers that life can bring a surprise.
Oh, no no! You're still not cross with your cute cuddly boy.
You'll go visit the pet shop, buy him some treats and another
puppy toy.
As he grows up he takes pride in obeying his master's voice.
He'll answer the door, bring your newspaper, what you
command him to do . . . is your choice.
Throughout your life together, he'll be your love and pride.
He'll be your loyal trusted friend and never leave your side.
In the game of life folk let you down bringing hurt your way.
You can always rely on man's best friend, a most treasured
friend - I'd say.

*Michele Simone Fudge*

# THE MUSIC MAKER

There's a little boy who lives in our street,
and to hear him it's a wonderful treat.
He plays the guitar like you've not heard before
and the music he plays everyone adores.
Though he's only ten he's a master it's true
he'll play rock and roll even a ballad for you.

He's so like a minstrel who's happy and gay
and never know different when you meet him each day.
Some say he's a genius and this may be so,
but he's not had the chance of stealing the show.
Though the time will come when he'll go on stage
it is then he will have everyone shouting with rage.

He'll be the greatest the world had known,
and his folks will be so proud of him back home.
They will think of the days when he was young
and the pleasure he gave to everyone.
For those days will be remembered as a fete,
and a challenge to make his life complete.

*Frederick Goff*

## NIGHTMARES

Nightmares are a mixed-up mash
there are some who the reasons thrash.
Wonder if as they delve into strange dreams
they too come apart - at their own seams.
For when the unusual happenings come
they do, of course, affect some,
who use their brains to good effect.
trying the various pieces - to collect.
To piece together - to make a whole
like mixing ingredients - in a bowl,
some gets spilled and falls on floor,
so I want scientists to explore
just what happens to those escaped bits
which leave us - on awakening - in frantic fits.
Perhaps if they could solve those powers so deep
I could then get . . . a good night's sleep!

*John L Wright*

# THE MILLENNIUM

Passage of time, majestic chasms
born on the wing.
Fleeting and greeting carried aloft
breathtaking moments make my heart sing.
The farmer and animals safe in the Croft
whispering messages repeatedly transformed.
Bringing a response to the beauty adorned
exciting thrills fill the air with frivolity.
Dancing and singing with jocular jollity.
Too much to comprehend
To soon . . . to end.

Wonderful moments and
emotional instances.
Man and his ambition
captured and matured.
Bubbling and bursting
the wave of integrity.
Calling and beckoning the
Universe with a smile.
Onward, onward, drives
the mechanism.
Through the seasons of the years.
Cranks the engine follows
the rustling wind.
Constantly striving constantly
gaining.
Winding and grinding
patiently waiting and
catching the light . . .

Colours and textures
to thrill and excite.
This old world beginning
and ending in a
mystery . . . and delight.

*Sarah Margaret Munro*

## THE KITTENS

Tilly loves the kittens
they sit and watch her eat.
'If we're very lucky
there'll be a bit of meat!'

'Mmm it all looks tasty.
I'm such a hungry puss.
Give her a nudge with your paw
or there won't be much for us!'

Eventually they get their treat
then scamper off to rest.
Mummy comes into the room,
'My goodness! What a mess!'

Food and crumbs everywhere
upturned cups and plates.
Dirty paw-marks here and there,
what will be their fate?

Meanwhile the kittens are busy
with a bouncy ball of wool.
'We must have some excitement
life can be so dull!'

'What are those two saying?'
I just want to play.
'Hey! Watch out! That ball of wool . . .
it's running away.'

'Yes . . . we will be kittens,
and that is nothing new.
Always up to something
no matter what you do!'

**Wendy Watkin**

## INVITATION TO THE DANCE

*Come to the dance,*
Let's have a ball.
*Here is your chance.*

I'm sure you could prance
Without e'er a fall.
*Come to the dance.*

It's no distance
We have the hall.
*Here is your chance.*

You'll feel in a trance,
Just answer the call.
*Come to the dance.*

It will enhance,
You'll feel ten feet tall!
*Here is your chance.*

You'll make friends perchance,
And that isn't all.
*Come to the dance.*
*Here is your chance . . .*

**Lola Perks-Hartnell**

## DEAR GWEN

Dear Gwen
You were always cheerful and gay
the sun is shining brightly now.
It's your kind of day, you would sit out
on your veranda you always had a tan.
None of us realised how much you missed your Stan.

You always had such lovely flowers on show,
they looked so nice from the street below.
I often wish that I could turn back the time
and sit with you once more.
Or we could walk together along
Southseas . . . sea shore.

*Sheila K A Thompson*

## ENID

We met occasionally
for a nice break.
Fresh coffee, hot toast
and salady things.
Flowers were sent
and poems were read.
What are 'phones for
but to communicate
the tenderest of things.
A robin sits
shivering and shaking
under the heavy sky.
Numbness disappears
when the rain
makes a heavy din.
Come red bird
and let us unite,
there are songs
to sing
this Christmas night . . .

*Tom Clarke*

## LAUGHTER

How can you write of laughter?
When so many cry.
How can you speak of laughter
when so many innocents die!

Faces of young children
etched in tears and pain.
Their laughter has been stolen,
do they weep in vain?

Cliffs washed over by the sea
are cleansed by waves no more.
Crude oil, gushing free
pollutes both sands and shore.

Devastated by man's greed
lying with feathers spoiled.
Seabird, wildlife, all in need,
their lovely plumage oiled.

Woman of Palestine scatter,
their dreams of peace no more.
Homes in ruins - shattered
among the spoils of war.

I can only write of sorrow
though my tears have been denied.
Will there be hope, tomorrow!
for today . . . the laughter died.

**William Price**

# YESTERDAY . . .

Yesterday I passed a young couple
kissing on the street
by the very same tree
where you and I used to meet.
There I remember,
I carved out your name
within a heart-shape for you
just saying I loved you.
Why is love like the dying leaf on the tree.
Love comes and love goes
with every beat of your heart.
The winter wind still calls out
your name to me.
Those stars said I loved you
with all of my heart.
Why then in love -
tonight . . . must we still be apart?

***K Lake***

## AUTUMN

Summer has gone and as winter draws near.
Most birds fly south - the winter they fear.
Little birds everywhere, have learnt to fly.
Then fly away from winter, for fear they should die.
The leaves turn brown and fall from the trees,
They are saying *goodbye* in the blustery breeze.
The mist in the morning, caresses the ground,
The dew is like teardrops, all scattered around.
For mother nature is crying *goodbye* to us all.
*'Will see you next spring, when my flowers are tall!'*

**I Baylis**

## PORTRAIT OF LIFE

Life paint many pictures
on a canvas of hope and dreams.
From a palette of mixed emotions
to create many magical scenes.
If calm, still and peaceful
it covers all aspects of life.
Mix in shadows of darkness
for explosions of fire and ice.

We see lots of shattered illusions
devoid from reason or rhyme.
Our painting is full of confusion
rife with violence and crime.
Gone is all peace and tranquillity
lost in the passing of time.
What's left is a selfish hostility
to take what is rightfully mine.

The painting of life is a mixture
of loving, or hating the most.
Some view a wonderful picture
others keep counting the cost.
Still the artist paints on regardless
even though his picture may fade.
One day, with fresh understanding
beauty will shine from the shade . . .

*Gig*

# I'M FOND OF THE PARK

Shy primroses appear first of all
then cheerful daffodils beneath the trees tall,
Which leafless still and dark
loom gauntly in the park.

Next, the camellia shrubs display
a riot of pink hues . . . Although the day
might be far from mild,
Often you see a mother and a child
strolling along the paths there,
Enjoying the early blooms and the fresh air;
the older children are at school.

In the middle of the park a large pool
is the favourite meeting place
For mallards, and young coots to race,
while a pair of resident swans patrols
the sedge-fringed waters; even curlew - calls
resound there at night, in the dark . . .
Yes! I'm very fond of the park!

*Daniela M Davey*

# THE LIVID WIFE . . .

She walked up the stairs towards an auspicious light
clutching herself with a painful twist.
And as she stared at the stranger in the bathroom mirror
her face reflected the patterns of his deadly fist.
Not knowing anymore whose image this belonged to
she stared at her soul through the darkness of her eyes.
She promised herself that she would see the sun again
as night arrived and darkness had engulfed the skies.

This time a disguise was not a necessary requirement.
She'd covered up the scars for much too long.
Instead she stood there naked with a hatred in her heart
swaying to the thought of some justifiable wrong.
Now she wasn't afraid to look at her livid body
as she wanted to reassure herself that *this* was her reality.
She opened up the door again, walking pure into the hall;
taking with her a raging past and leaving behind her sanity.

With chocolates and flowers he lay there drunk on the couch.
As she wandered to the kitchen with a nonplussed mind
she searched with blankness for her accompanying friend
which after fifteen years, she finally did find.
So she only did what she thought she was supposed to.
She only did what any desperate woman could.
She raised up death and struck with it her enemy.

But I'll not pretend I don't remember.
The blood . . . the blood!

***Louise Gallagher***

## A CRAZY LOVE?

*(For Hannah, Chris, Magda)*

*M* was Polish
Polish and crazy
Polish and crazy as a loon
By night
she lived above the TV Repair Shop
and by day
she taught at the local school.
I don't know what she taught there,
but I bet my sweet pension
she was damn fine . . .

*Chistophe* rode into town
all the way from North Marton.
Worked the circus there
fought tigers
butted alligators
made the tea.
They were both crazy
both good crazy
and I take good crazy
over crazy, crazy
any old time . . .

*Christophe* was raised
on good ale
and bad football pitches.
*M* was raised
on Lech Warlenska
and Volvo cars.
*Christophe's* dreams
were psychedelic
*M's* were
Gdansk grey . . .

But *Cupid*
is the craziest bastard of all
and not distance
nor logic
nor fine ales
nor square cars
muddy fields or bad moustache's
cut any ice with the naked un
and I
for one
*like it that way* . . .

**Simon Green**

## SNIPPITS

'Coughs and sneezes spread diseases!'
Wartime posters said.
For doctors knew a dose of flu
Meant seven days in bed.

The safety poster on the wall
Seemed incomplete to him.
'Think!' was all the poster said
So he added 'Or Thwim!'

'Ships are safest here!' he said,
'In harbour, at their ease.
But ships are made to ply their trade
Out there in stormy seas.'

Opinions differ over whether
TV is a boon.
But what a thrill, that day, to watch
Man walking on the moon.

It's said a dog is man's best friend,
Not all agree with that.
The perfect friend is, some contend,
A lazy fireside cat.

'I've seen the mist,' the climber said
'Above the mountains green.'
His friend, who'd stayed behind replied
'Too bad I've missed the scene!'

*Frank Jensen*

## THE HERO

Her arms were flailing in the air
the sea was rough - the currents tough.
It was too much for her to bear,
going down fighting she'd had enough.

She couldn't swim another stroke
as tiredness overwhelmed her.
Wave upon wave over her head broke.
On giving up she felt some fur . . .

She saw the lovely eyes at first
then grabbed the animal's collar.
It felt as though her lungs would burst
pulling her out of this horror.

***Beulah Thompson***

## AWARENESS

Fairy children laugh and play.
Poppy chasing them every day.

Miniature laughter fills the air
the cat engaged in a game of stare.

Glittering lights all around.
Elfin magic is abound.

Protecting Greenwood all the way
let nature spirits have their say.

Mischief makers they must be,
yet all will guard each and every tree.

Return the service they have done
plant a tree and tell your son.

The air we breathe will depend on this
send every nature spirit a kiss.

When all declare Mother Nature Queen
they will let themselves be seen.

Not forgetting Father Nature king
while all their praises we may sing.

***Deborah Hall***

## THERE IS ONLY FEAR . . .

So here I am in a laboratory
I've got electrodes in my brain.
Can I have a biscuit?
If you torture me again I'll p\*\*s on your shoes
(made from leather - I knew the owner!).
I touched someone's tit,
so the Police decided to experiment on me.
Was kicked about a bit,
but I'm only a fat cat, businessman, laboratory rat.

*Paul Desca*

## STANTON REVISITED

October, October, kaleidoscope of colour,
Glad, glad day retrospective of summer,
Returning to the Eden of happy childhood,
Amidst radiant hills remembered in youth.

Closer I approached with bated breath
To my dreamland, Oh! How my heart leapt,
Of sunlit stone, and that first glimpse
Of purple flowers in a wall's crevice.

Lighter my footsteps on the upward way,
Breathless with urgency I paused midway,
Through a gateway, coming face-to-face
With paradise lost, to the hills' embrace.

Love overwhelming, senses deep aroused,
Past swiftly relived, feel heart pound,
Towards forest hastening, into darkness
Alone with thoughts, not with loneliness.

Into heart's haven came body and soul,
Wondrous creation in act of renewal,
Tears on the ground replenishing Earth,
All lay silent, not a sound was heard.

Nothing stirred but the swaying of trees,
Keepers of secrets, and decaying leaves,
Consummation's act, and giving of birth,
But all must die, be returned to Earth.

*Betty Mealand*

## IT IS NOT GOOD TO CRY NOW . . .

I could have done better with my life
but I did not understand at that particular time.
I was too young and inexperienced of anything.
With the time that goes by does it make any of us wiser?
But still I was wrong for not doing what I desired and wanted
                                        at the proper moment.
Very often I said to myself 'Do it tomorrow or next month.'
That was my biggest wrong, because what you can't do today
                                        you never do tomorrow!
We humans have never learned how to live on this Earth.
Only a few do what they wish and do as they please!
I think they have been the wise ones.
I cannot got back - my time has gone and has passed.
What is the regret for me now?
I am too old to rectify all my stupid mistakes of the past.
I have written this poem for the young people of the present day.
To tell them to think very hard before they waste their life - as I did!
It is no good crying now, I won't get back my lost time.
Enjoy life when you can . . . because soon life comes to an end!

*Antonio Martorelli*

# A DISTANT HARMONY

I saw you through the mists of time
and rose above my fear
To where the spirit guided me
in this uncommon sphere

I recognised the light within
it shone there in your eyes
A ray of hope cut through the dark
and caught me by surprise

Your voice, a distant harmony
upon the lips of love
A gentleness that flew upon
the white wings of a dove

You played this harp that is my heart
the melody was sweet
I felt the thaw of loneliness
the warmth of passion's heat.

*Kim Montia*